AF440484

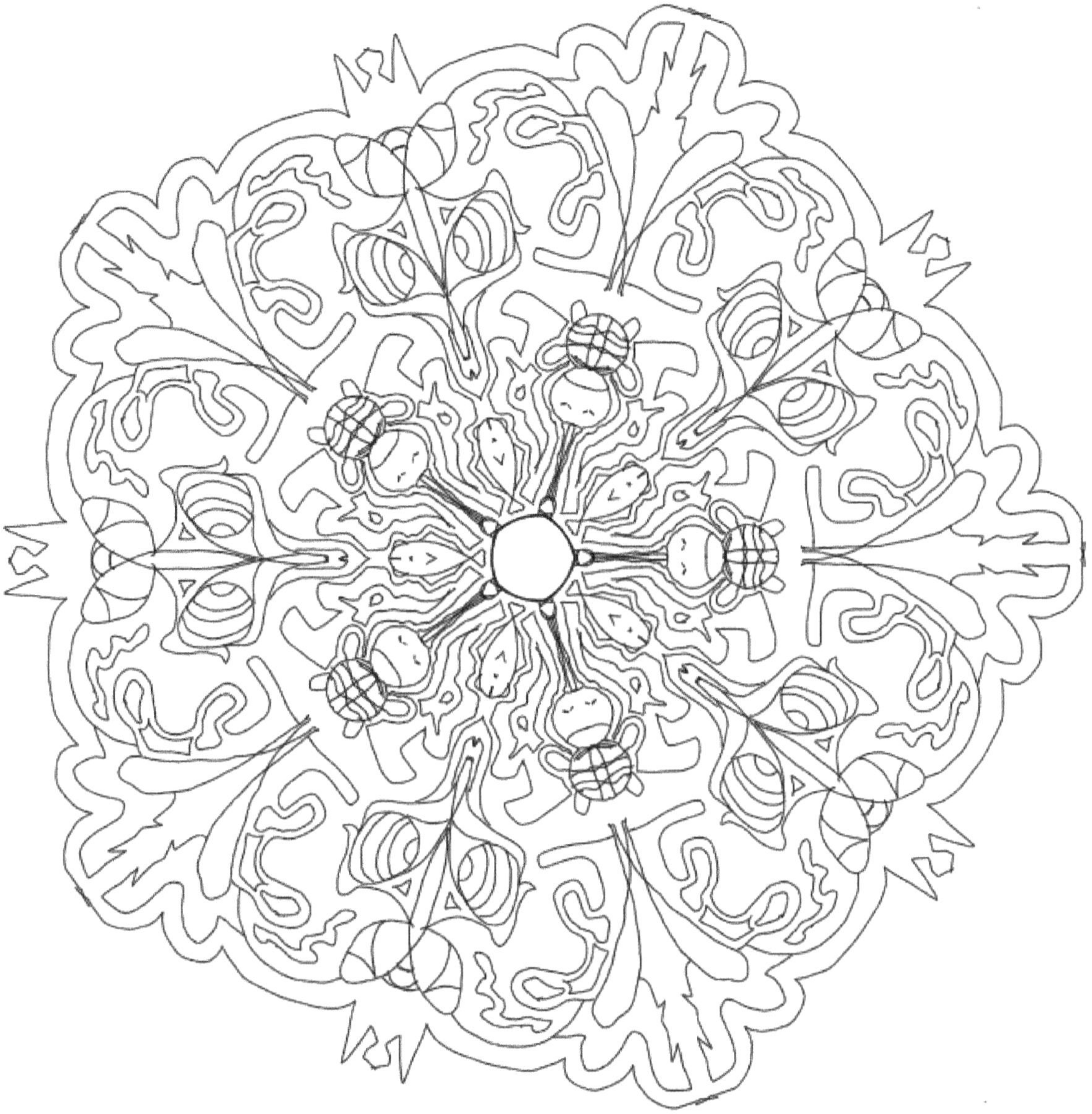

"Forget not
that the earth
delights
to feel your bare feet
and the
winds
long to play with
your hair."

~Khalil Gibran

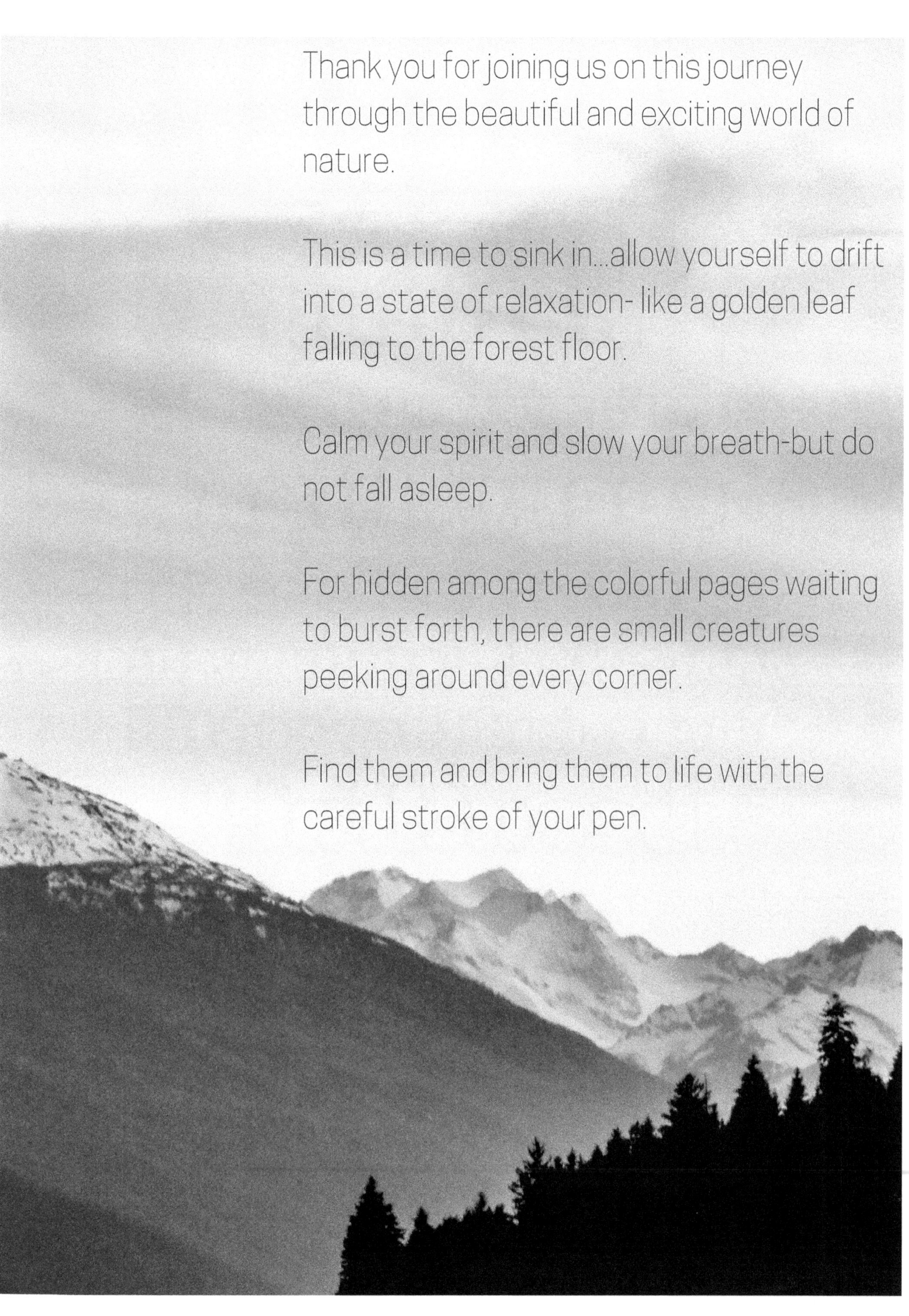

Thank you for joining us on this journey through the beautiful and exciting world of nature.

This is a time to sink in...allow yourself to drift into a state of relaxation- like a golden leaf falling to the forest floor.

Calm your spirit and slow your breath-but do not fall asleep.

For hidden among the colorful pages waiting to burst forth, there are small creatures peeking around every corner.

Find them and bring them to life with the careful stroke of your pen.

"In nature, **nothing** is perfect and **everything** is perfect. Trees can be contorted, bent in weird ways, and they're still **beautiful.**"

~Alice Walker

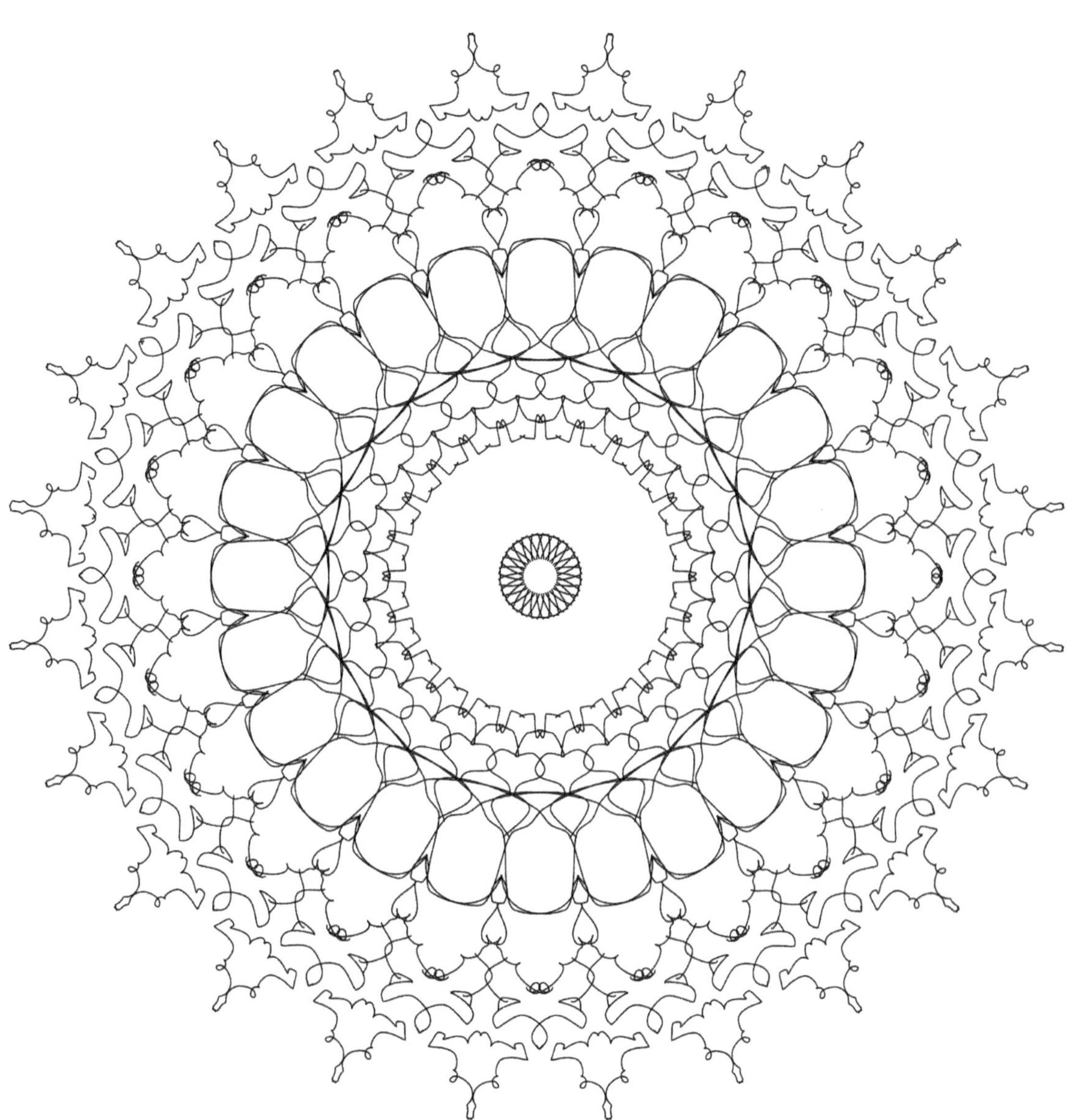

"Look
deep
into nature,
and then you will
understand
everything better."

~Albert Einstein

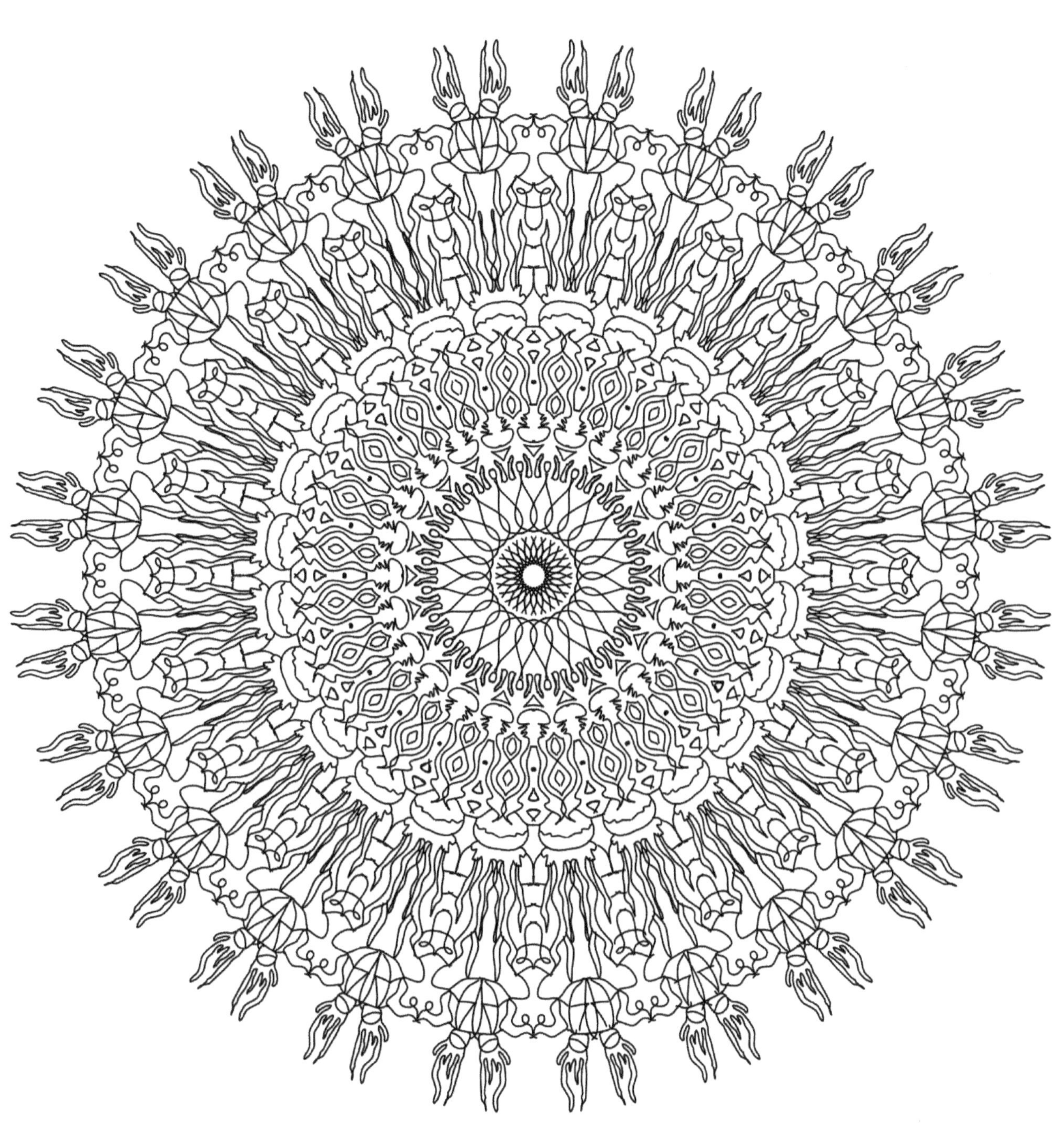

"Heaven
is under our feet
as well as over our
heads."

~Henry David Thoreau

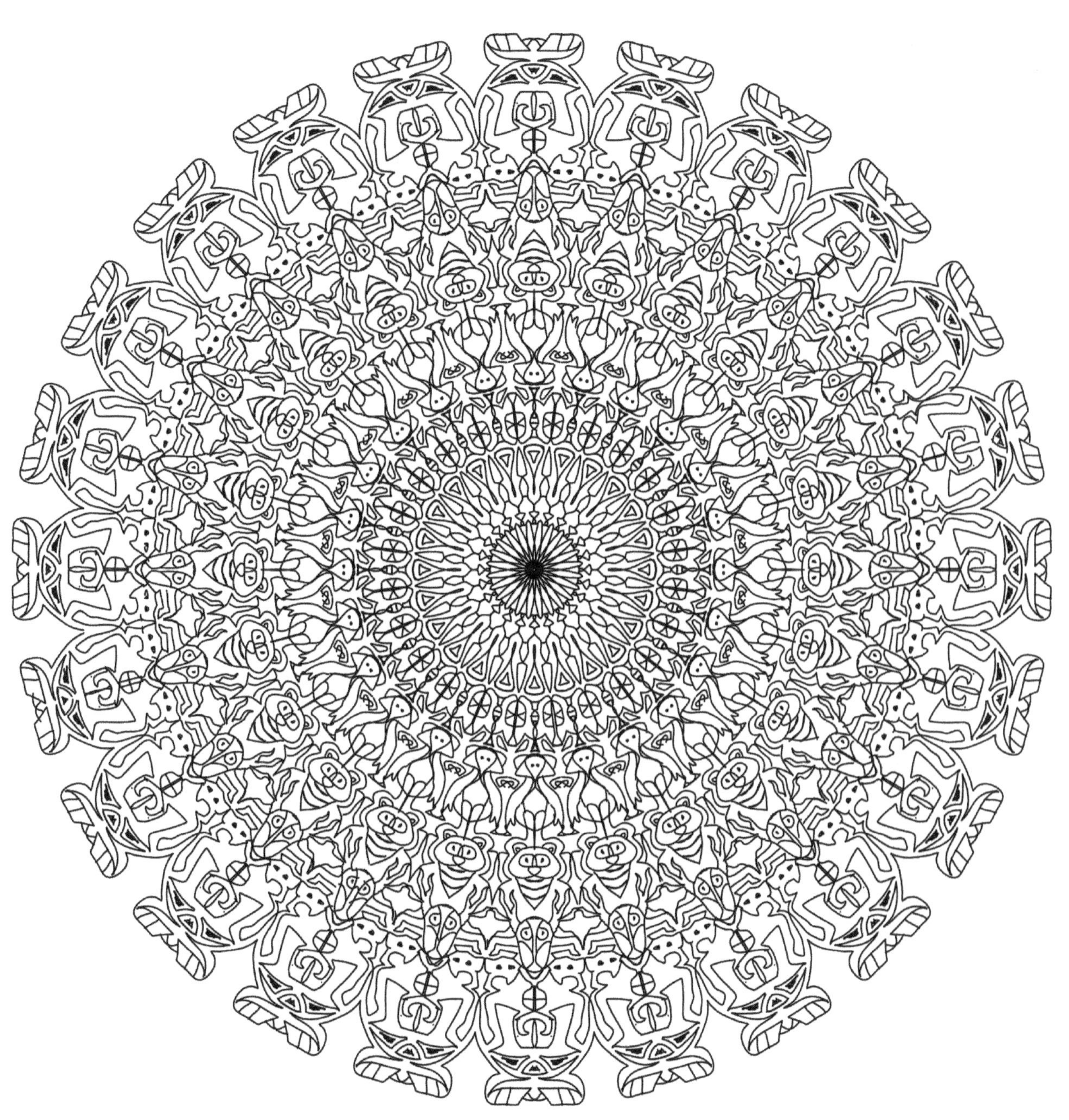

"To me a
lush
carpet of pine needles
or spongy grass
is more
welcome
than the most luxurious
Persian Rug."

~Helen Keller

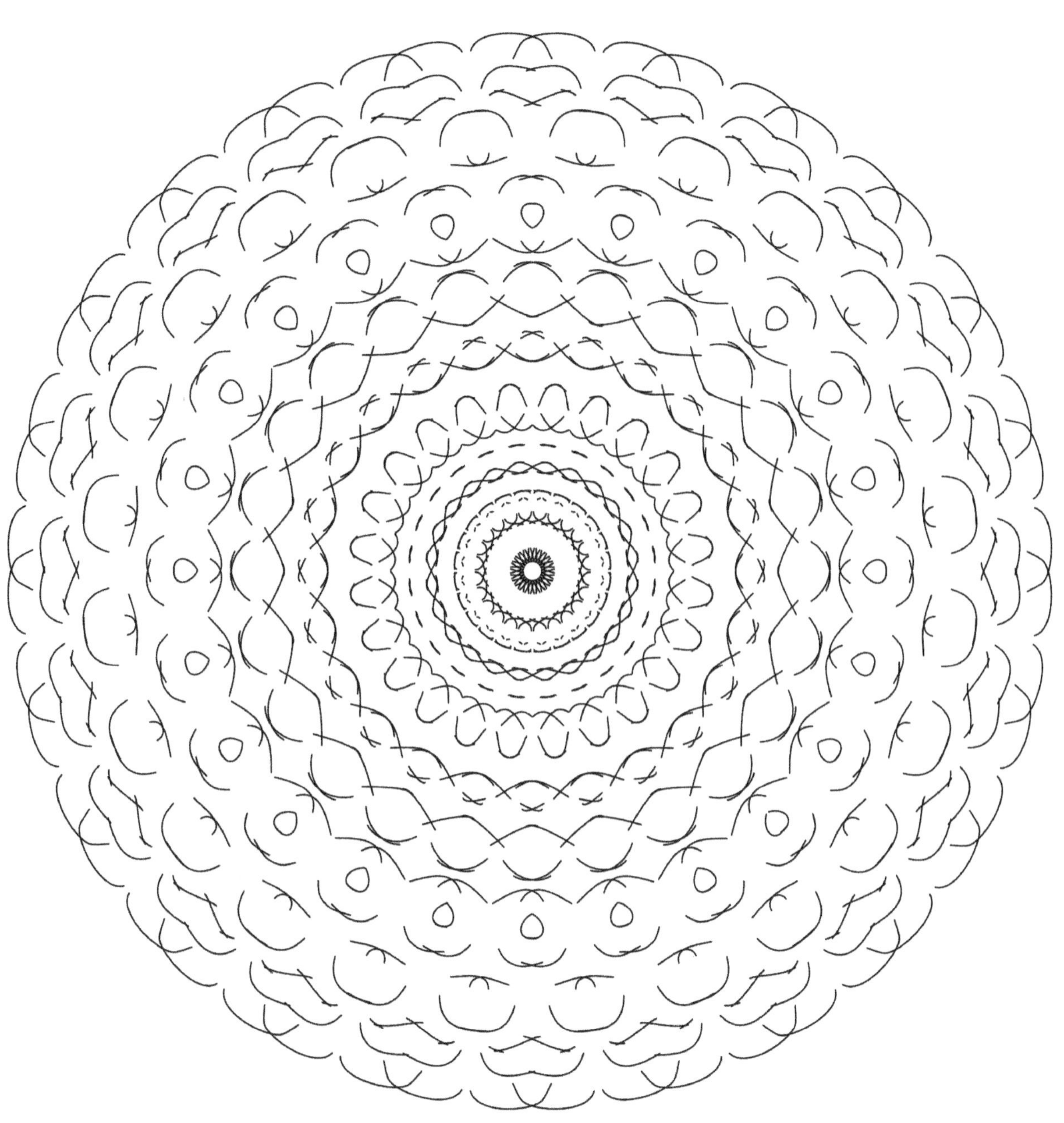

"We don't **inherit** the earth from our ancestors, we **borrow** it from our children."

~Native American proverb

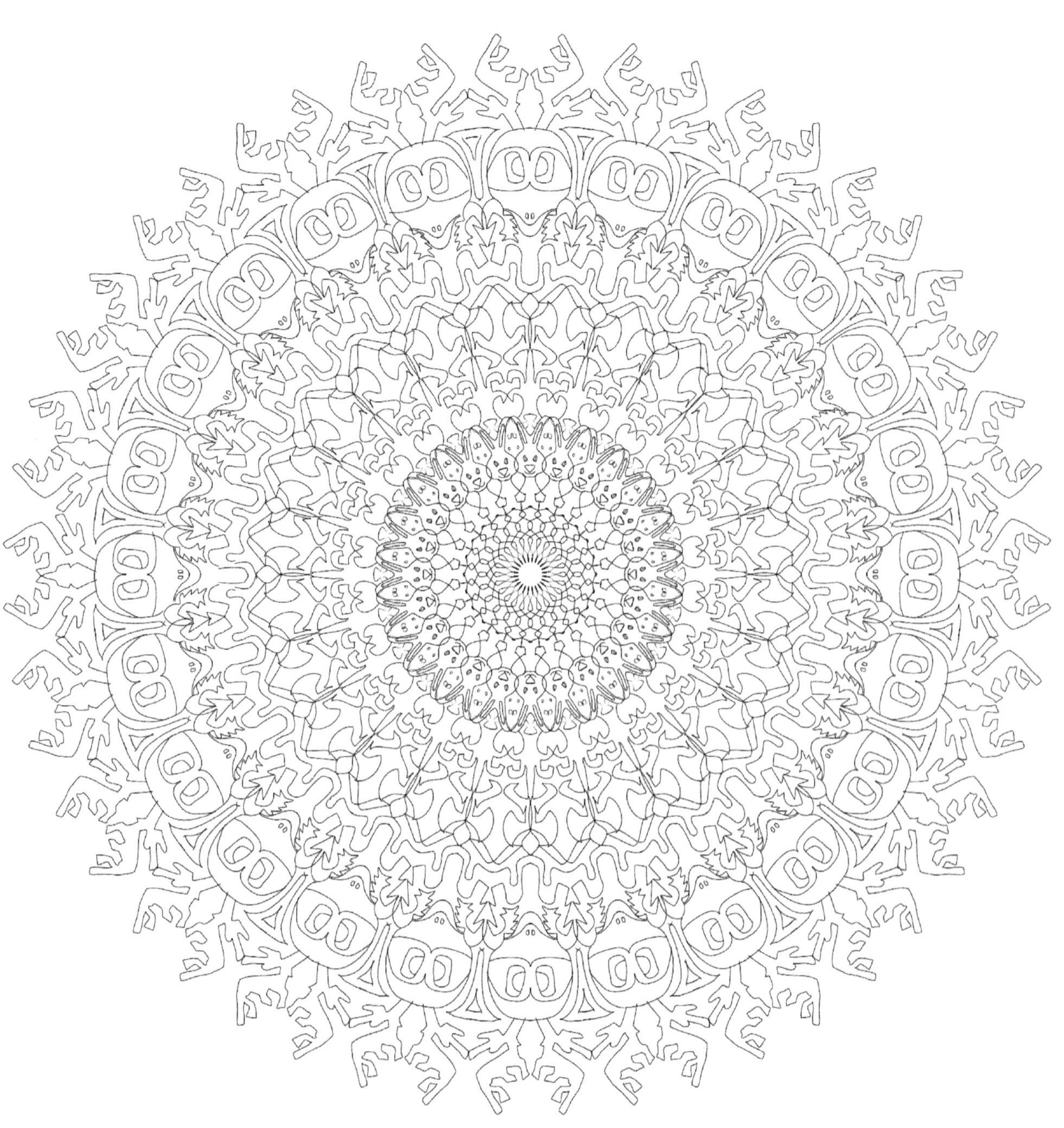

"Nature does not **hurry,** yet everything is **accomplished.**"

~Lao Tzu

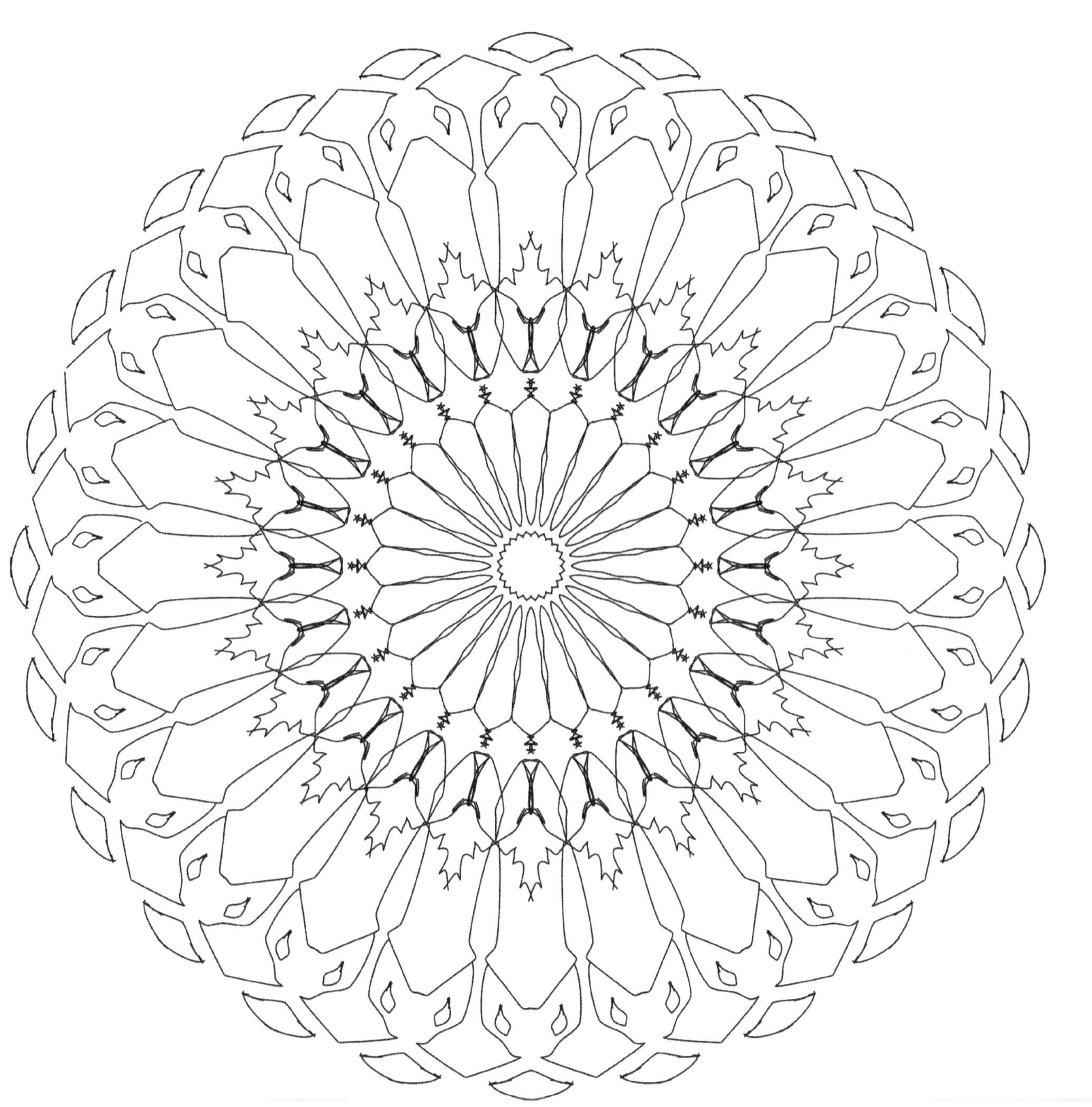

"If you truly **love** nature, you will find **beauty** everywhere."

~Laura Ingalls Wilder

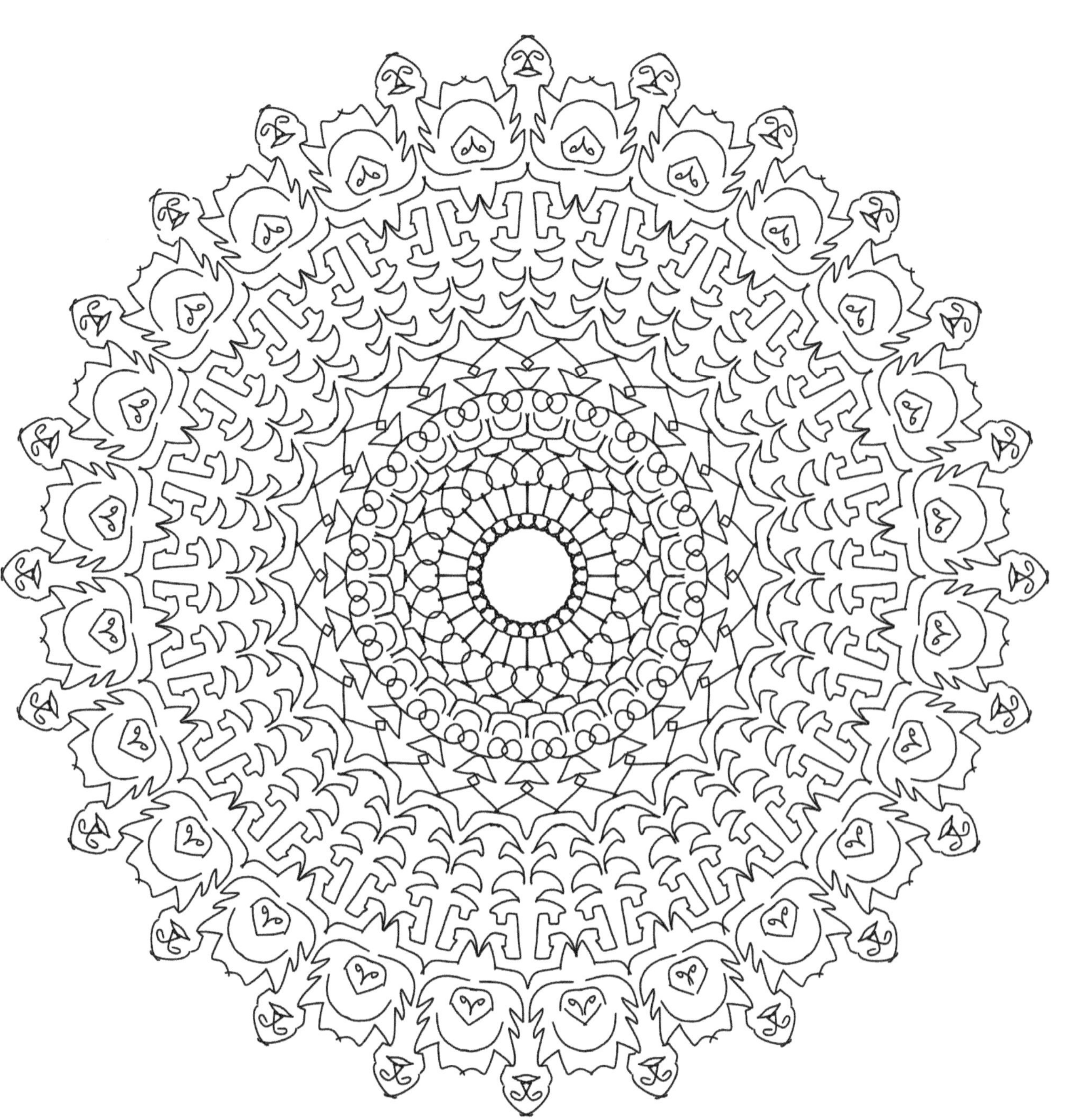

"There is something infinitely

healing

in the repeated

refrains

of nature - the assurance that

dawn

comes after night, and

spring

after winter."

~Rachel Carson

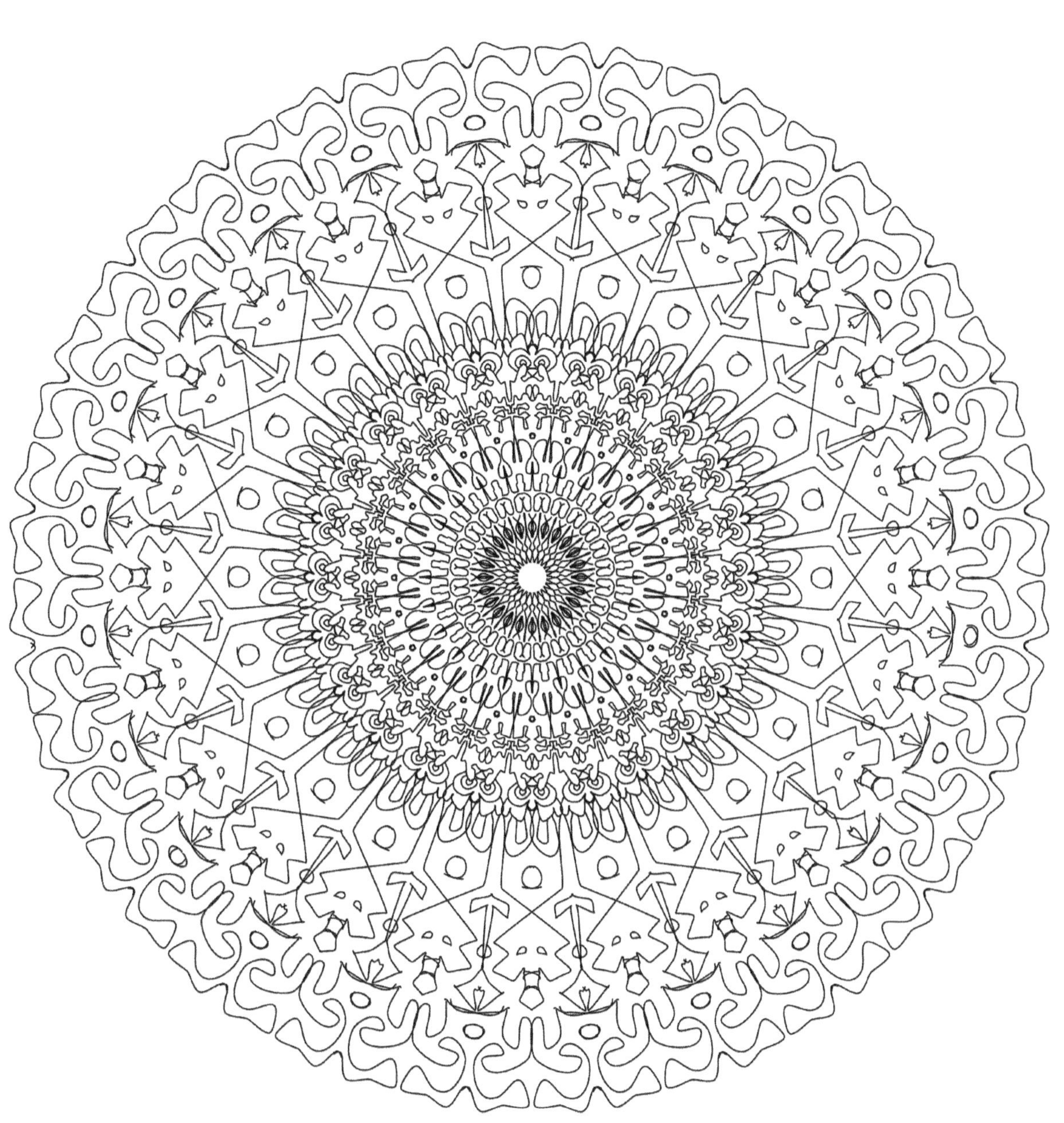

"Leave the **road,** take the **trails.**"

~Pythagoras

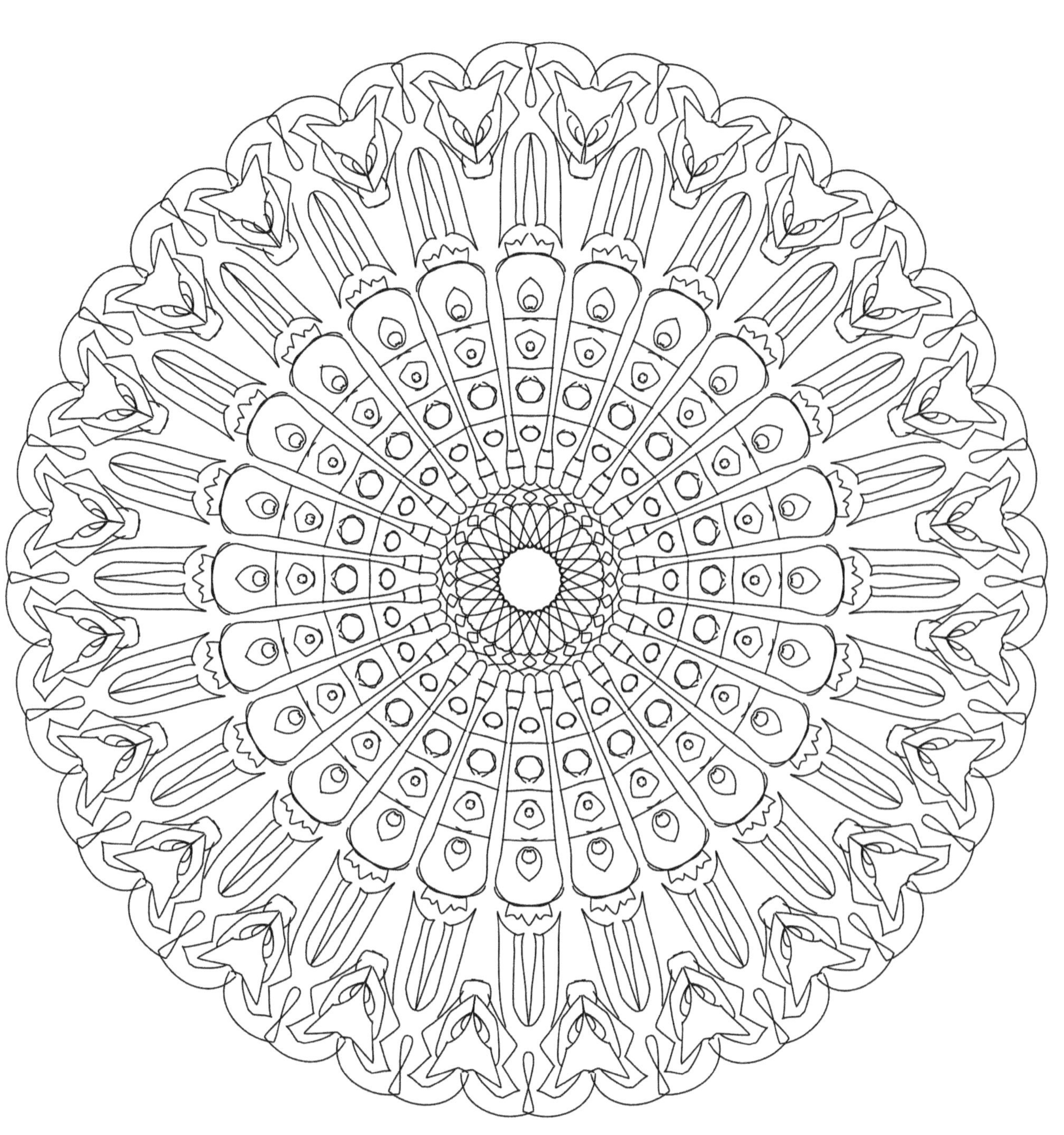

"Live
in each season
as it passes;
breathe the air,
drink the drink,
taste the fruit, and
resign
yourself to the
influence
of the earth."

~Henry David Thoreau

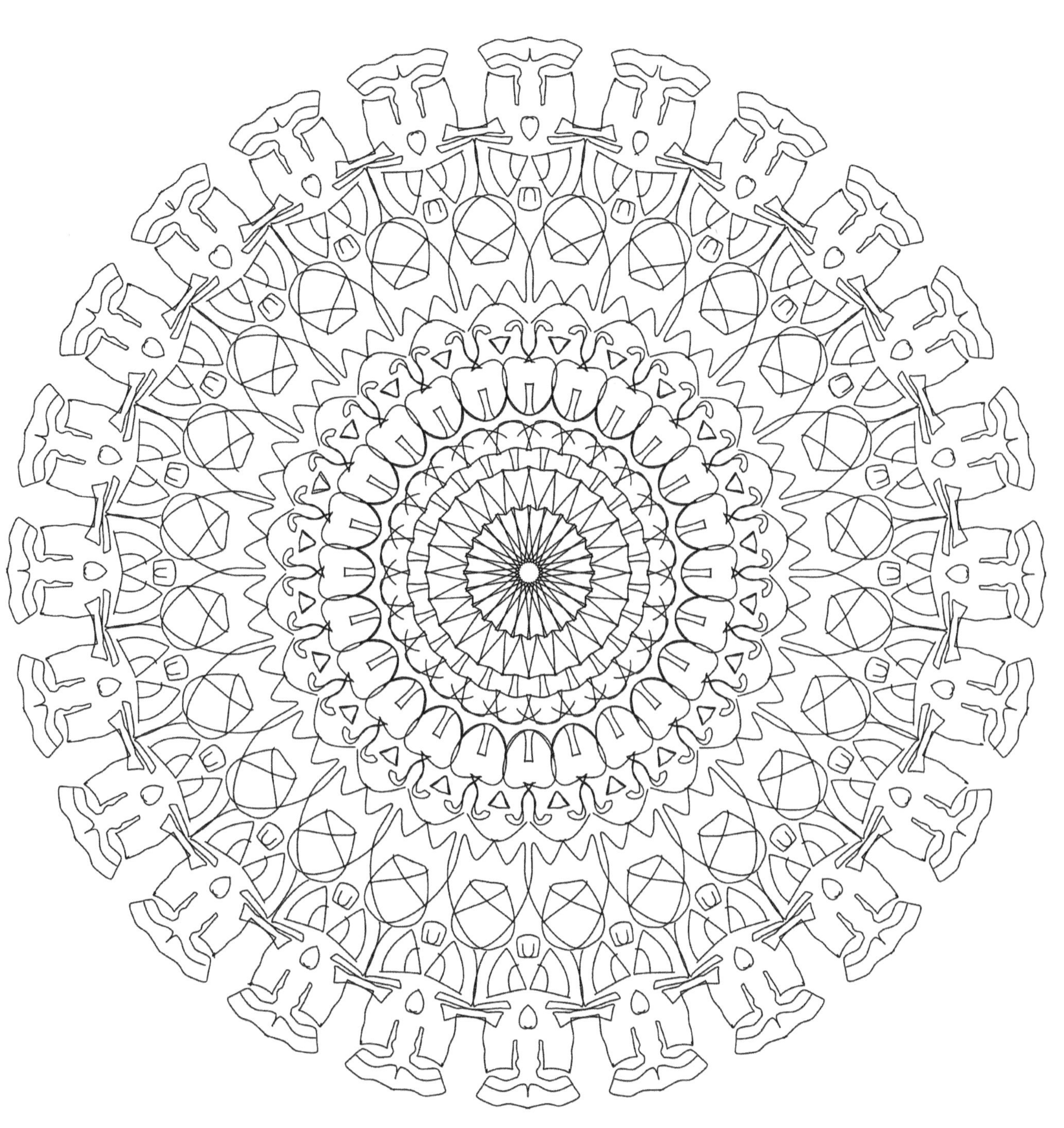

"I go to nature to be

soothed

and

healed,

and to have my

senses

put in order."

~John Burroughs

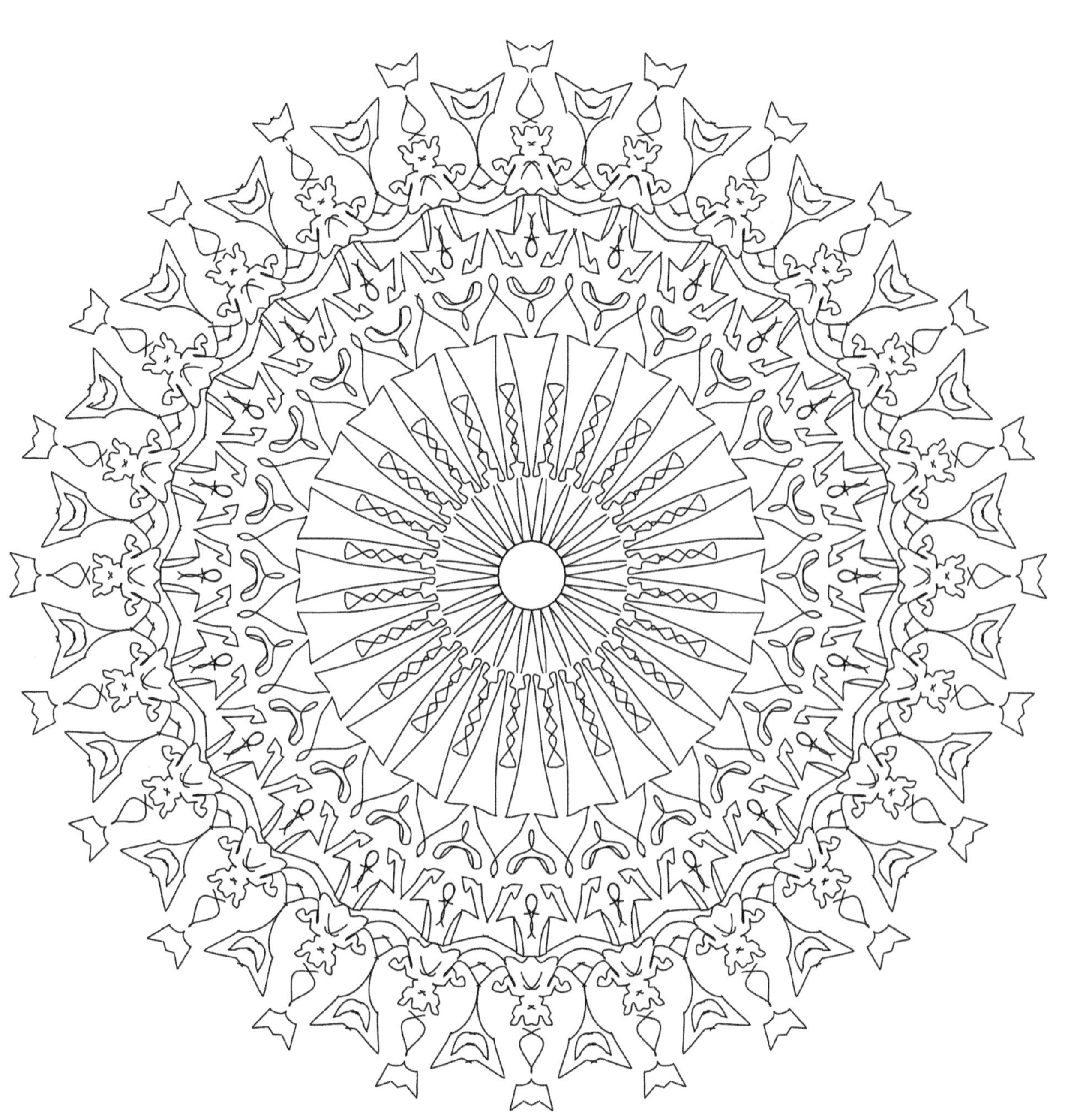

"For most of history,
man has had to
fight
nature to survive;
in this century
he is beginning
to realize that,
in order to
survive,
he must
protect it."

~Jacques-Yves Cousteau

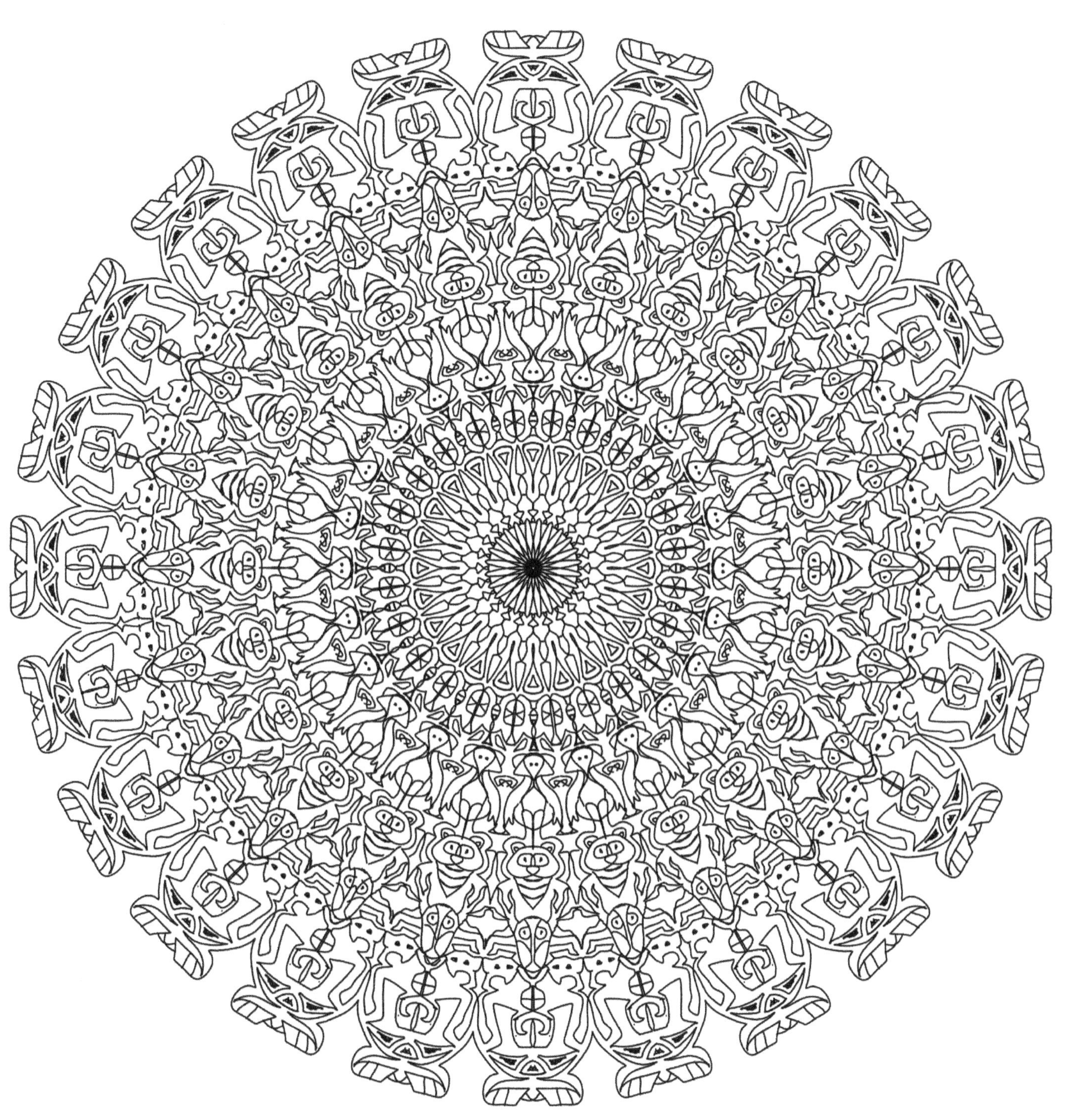

"There's a whole **world** out there, right **outside** your **window.** You'd be a fool to **miss it.**"

~Charlotte Eriksson

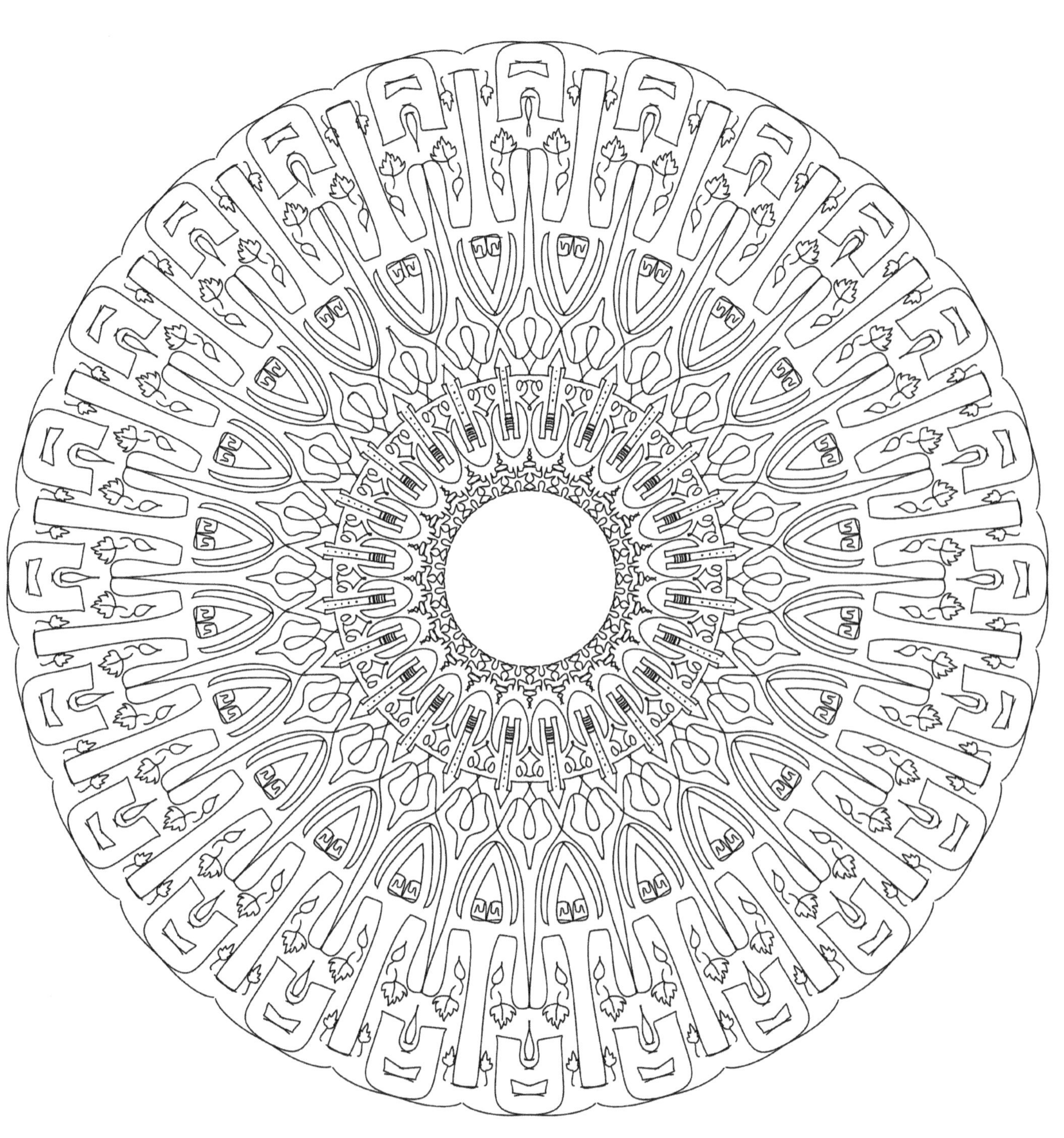

"To forget how to
dig
the earth
and to tend the
soil
is to forget
ourselves."

~Mahatma Gandhi

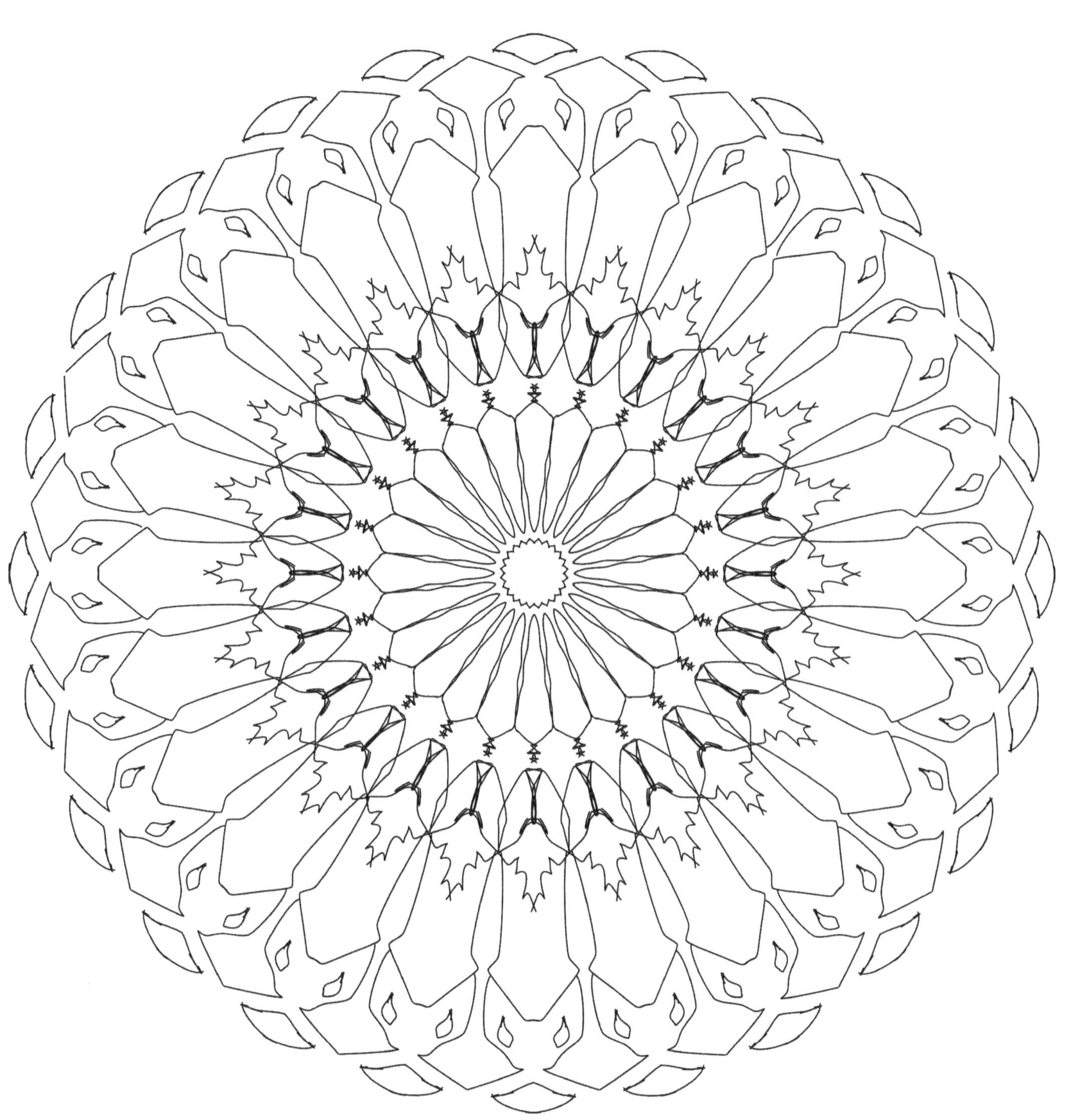

"Preserve

and

cherish

the pale blue dot,

the only

home

we've ever known."

~Carl Sagan

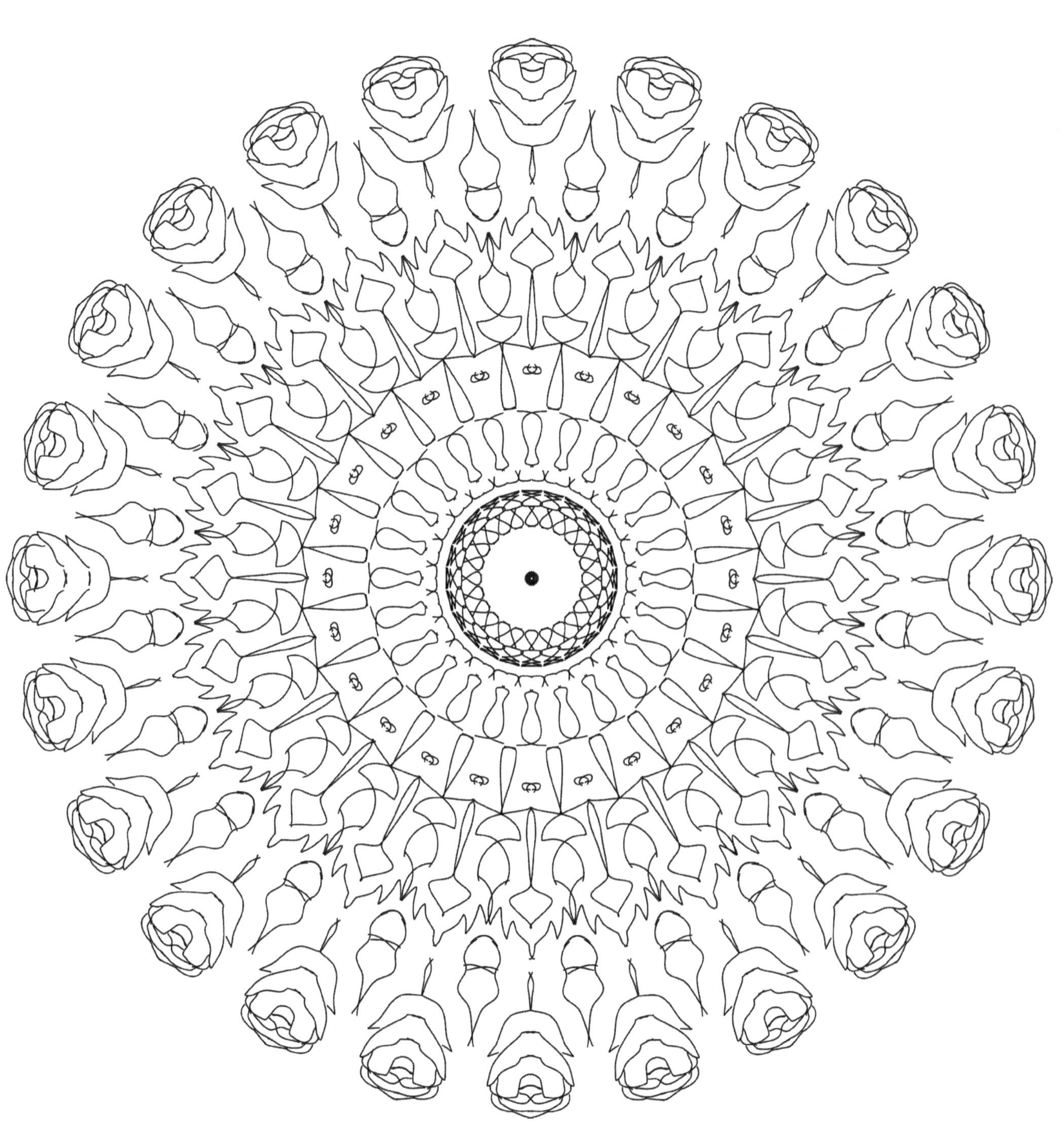

"Study nature, love nature, stay close to nature. It will never fail you."

~Frank Lloyd Wright

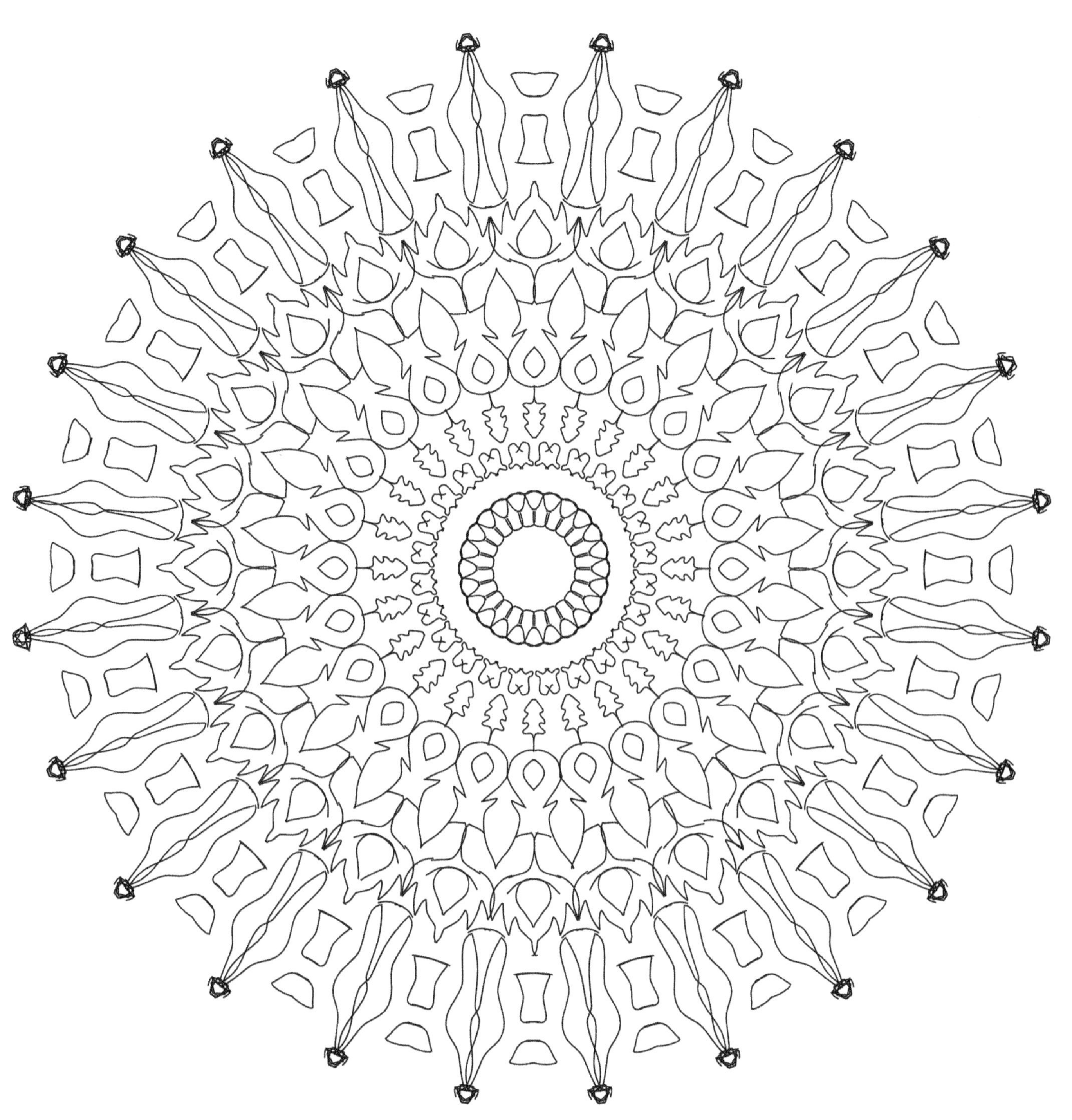

"The sun, with all those planets revolving around it and dependent on it, can still ripen a bunch of grapes as if it had nothing else in the universe to do."

~Galileo Galilei

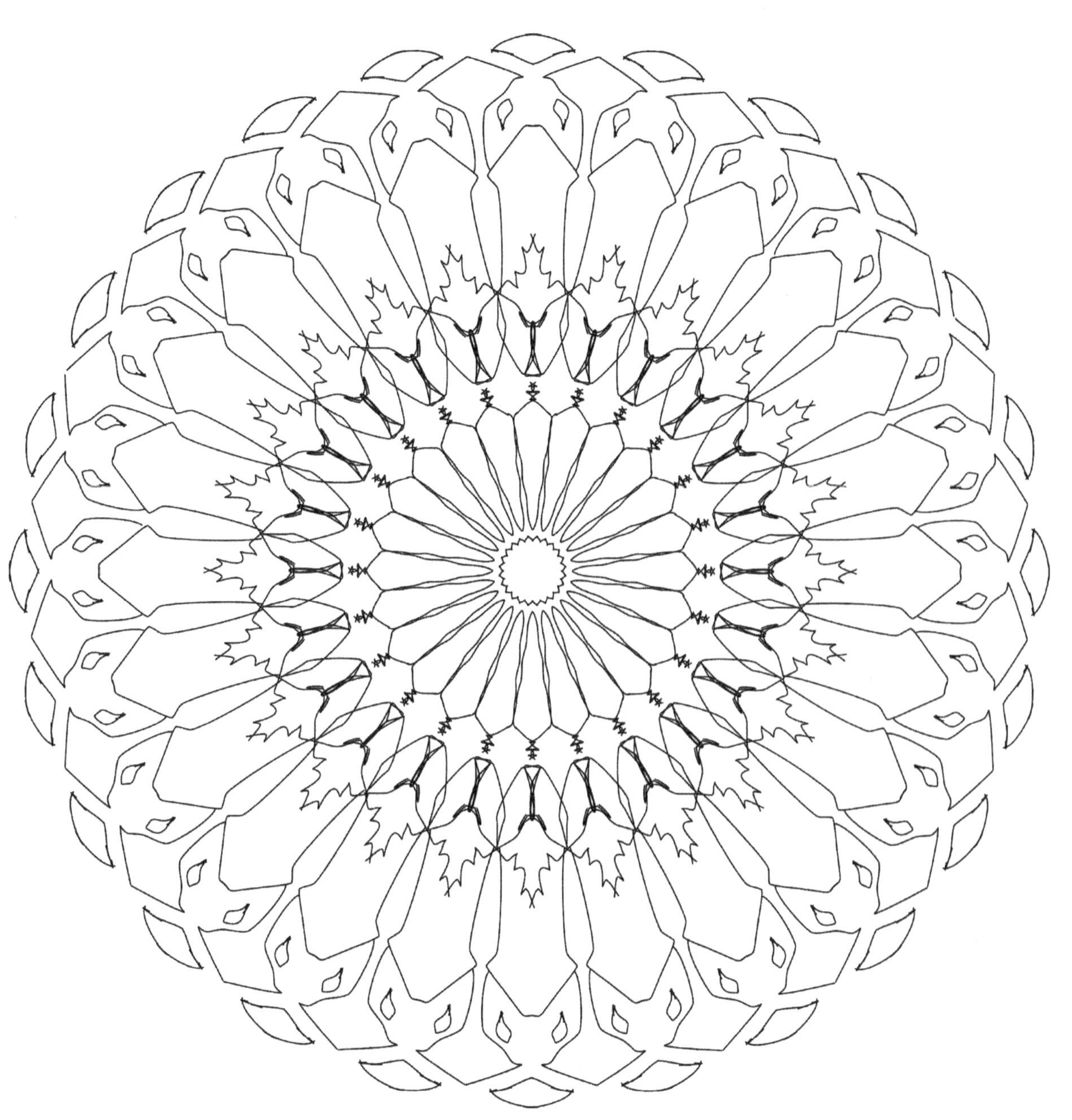

"All my life through, the **new** sights of **Nature** made me **rejoice** like a child."

~Marie Curie

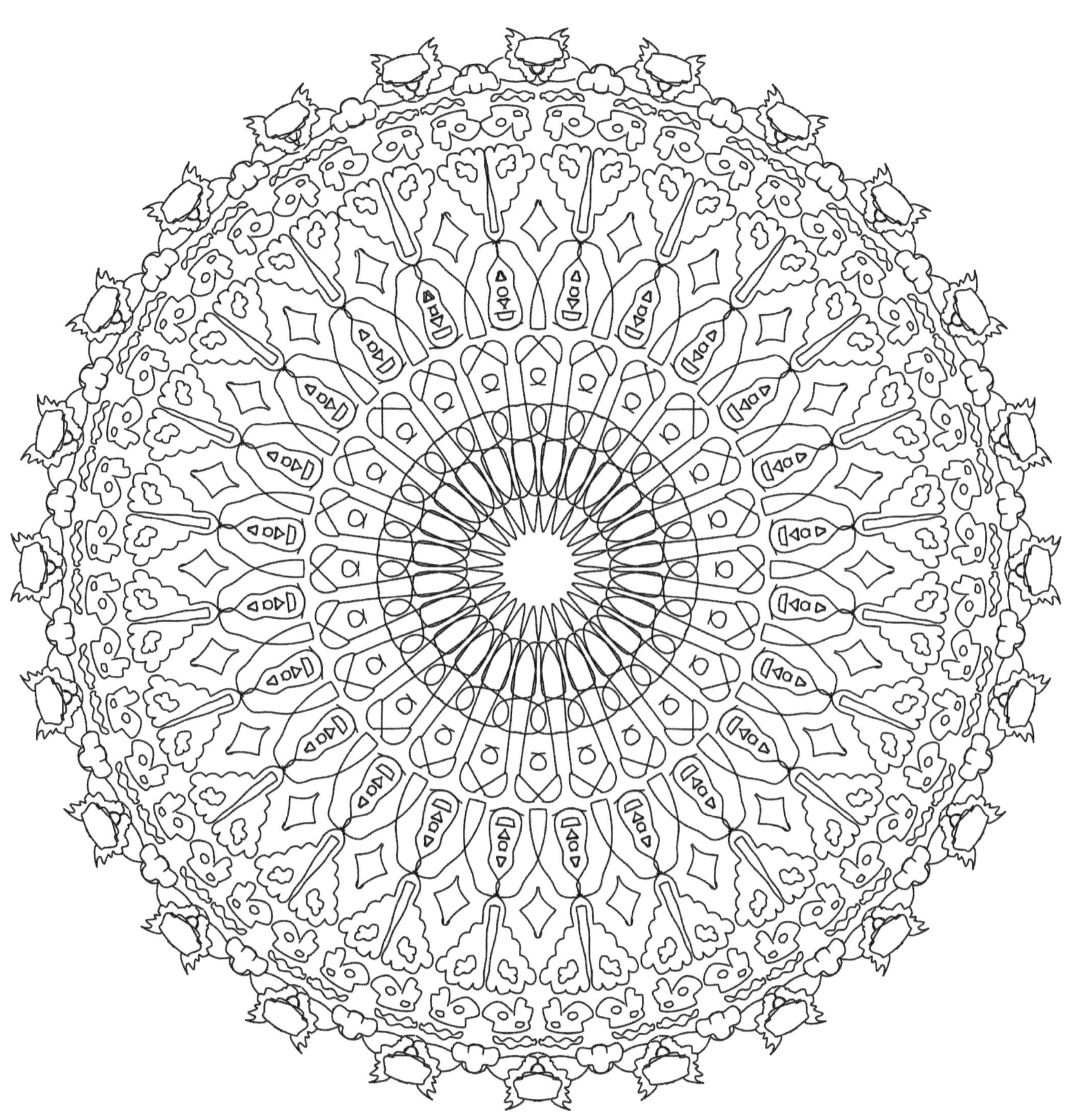

"Colors
are the
smiles
of nature."

~Leigh Hunt

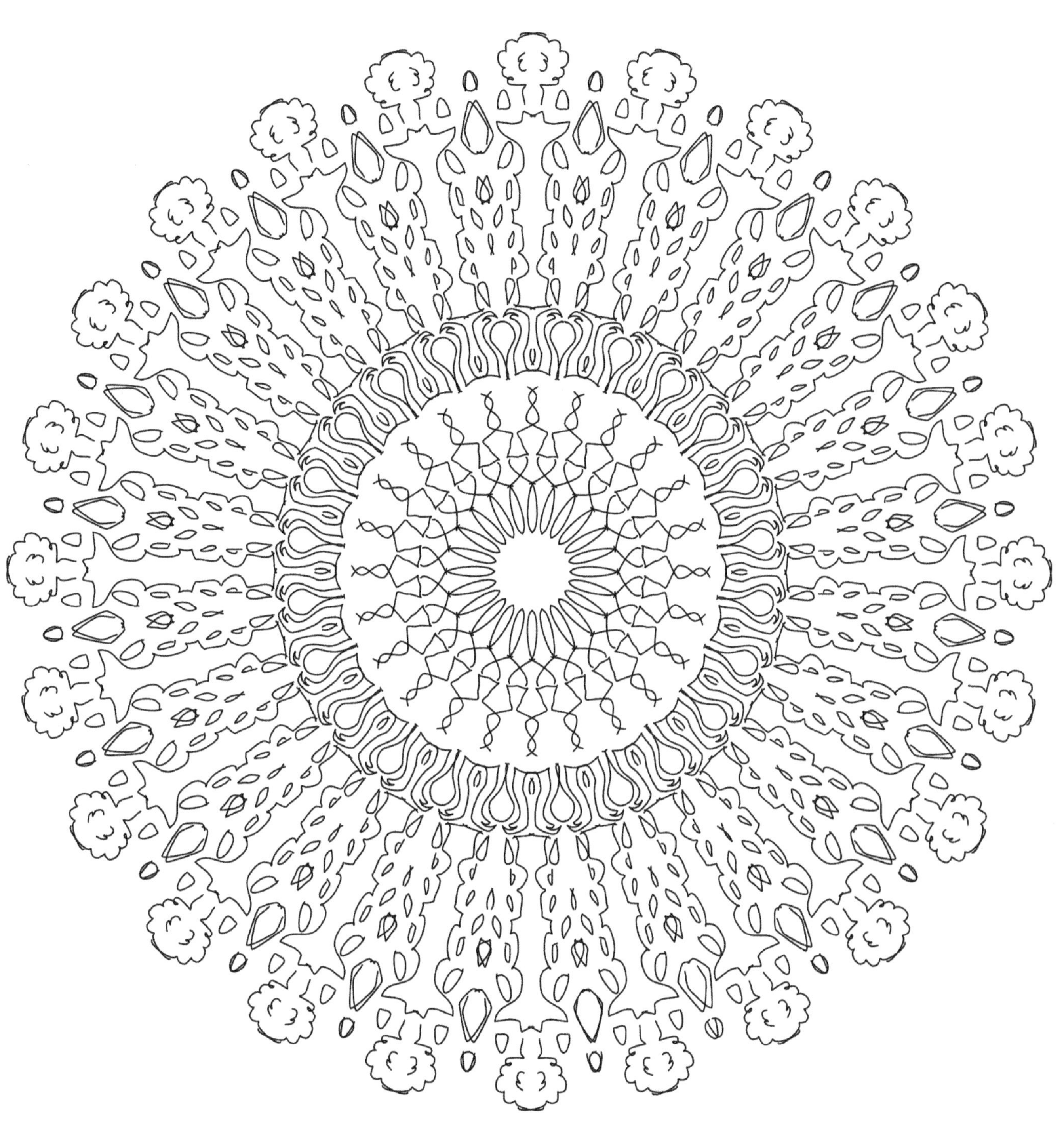

"Everything in nature

invites

us constantly

to be

what we are."

~Gretel Ehrlich

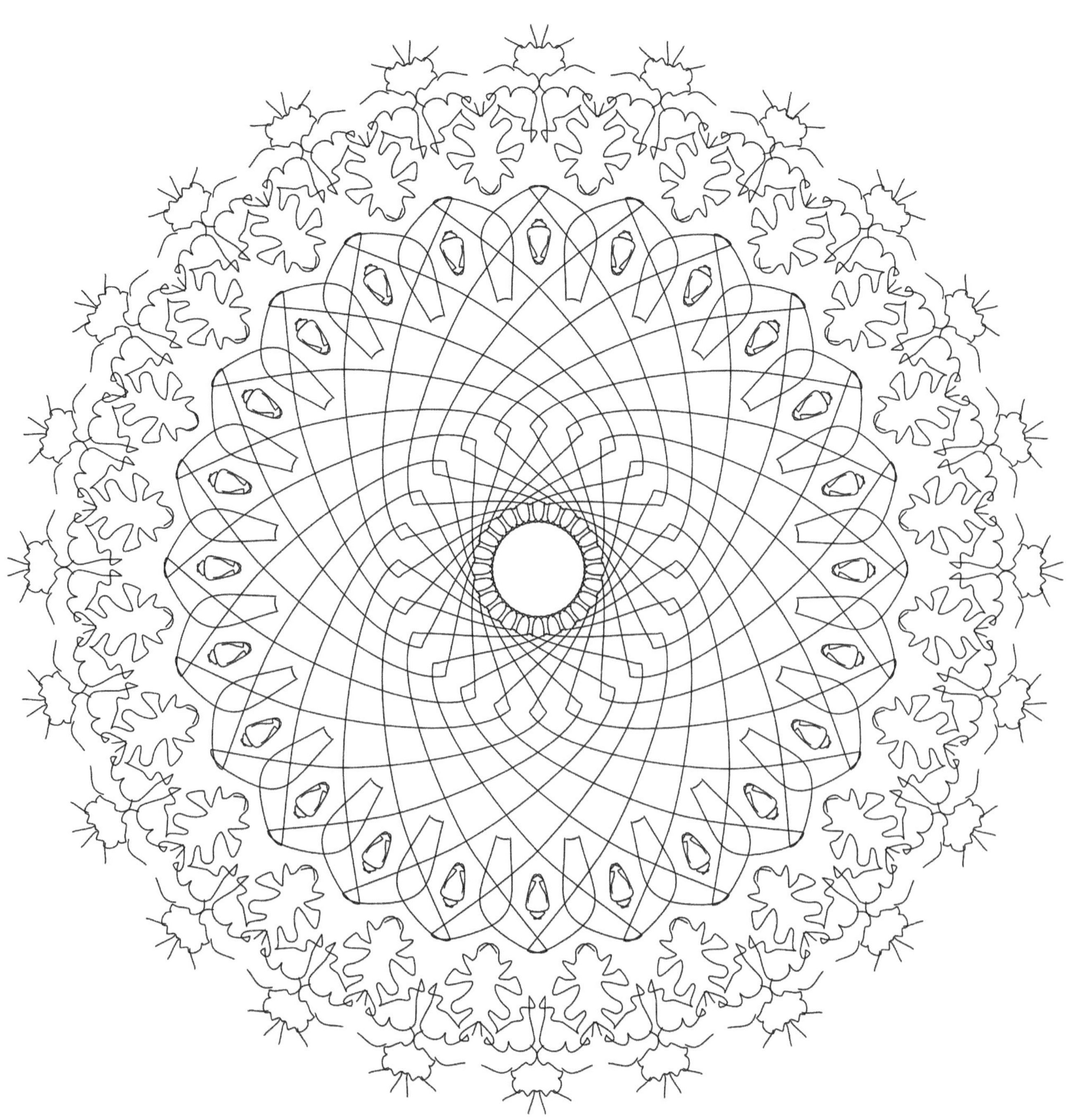

"The best thing
one can do when it's
raining
is to let it
rain."

~Henry Wadsworth Longfellow

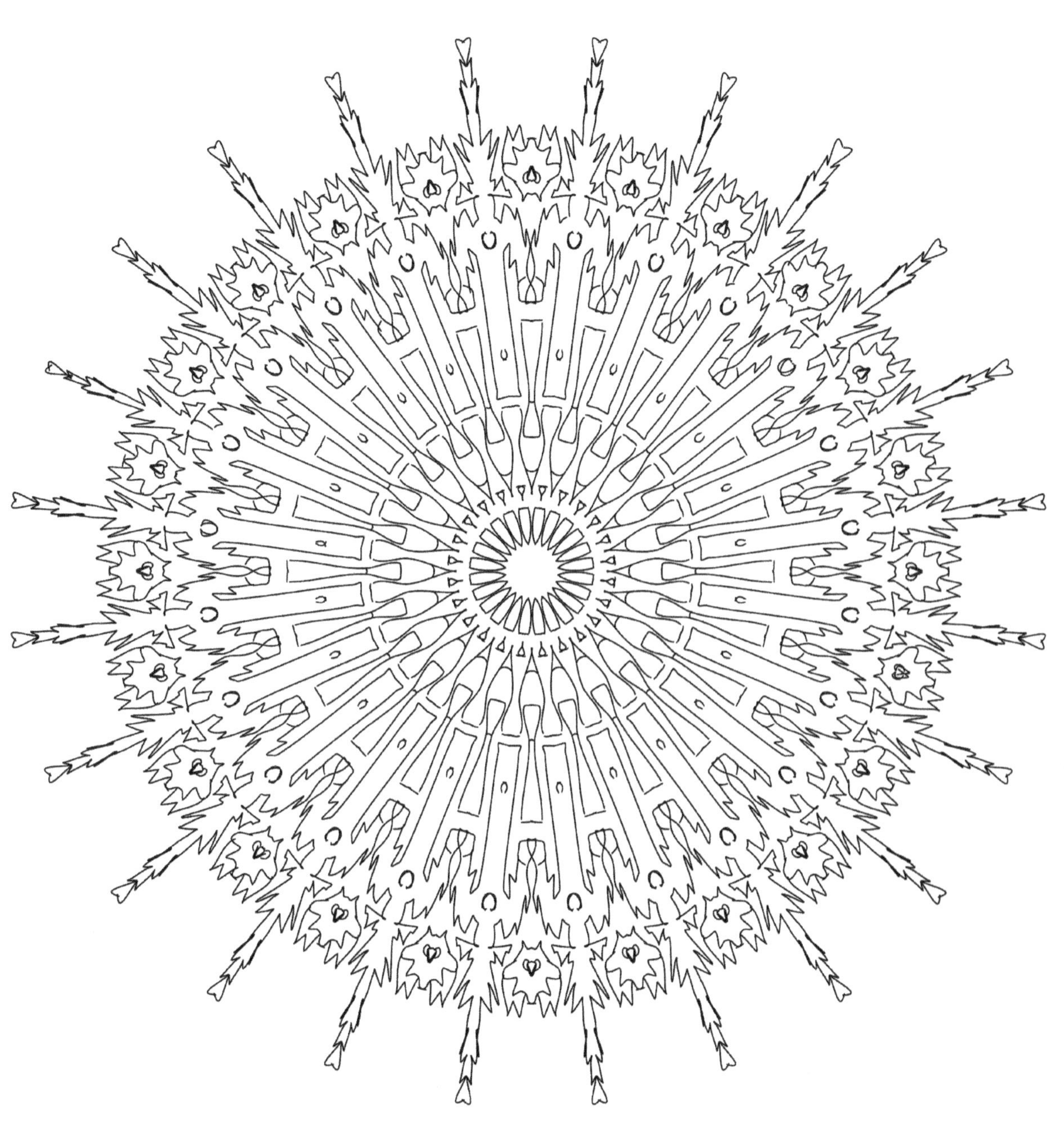

"Many eyes go **through** the meadow, but **few** see the **flowers** in it."

~Ralph Waldo Emerson

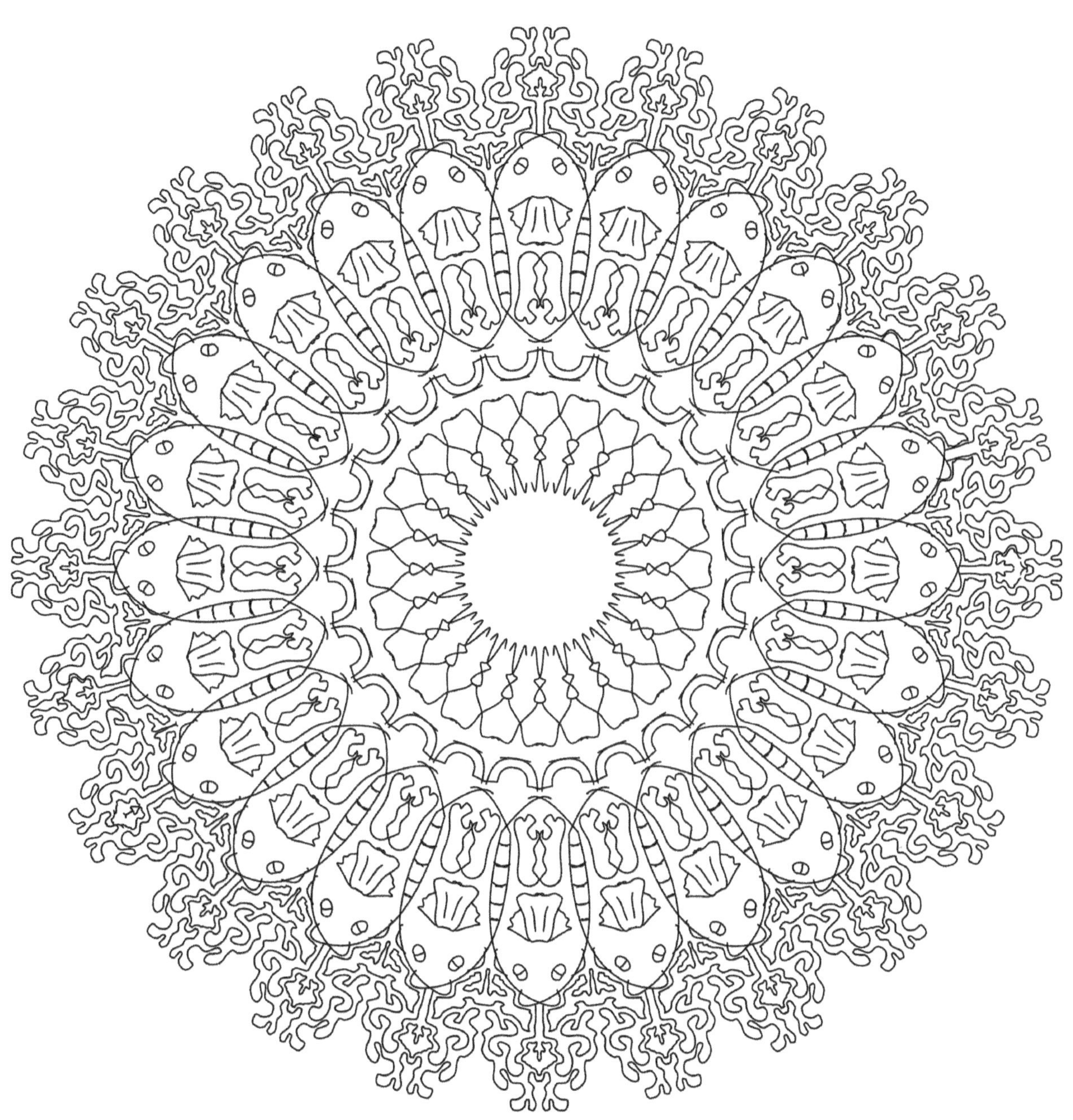

"Real **freedom** lies in **wildness,** not civilization."

~ Charles Lindbergh

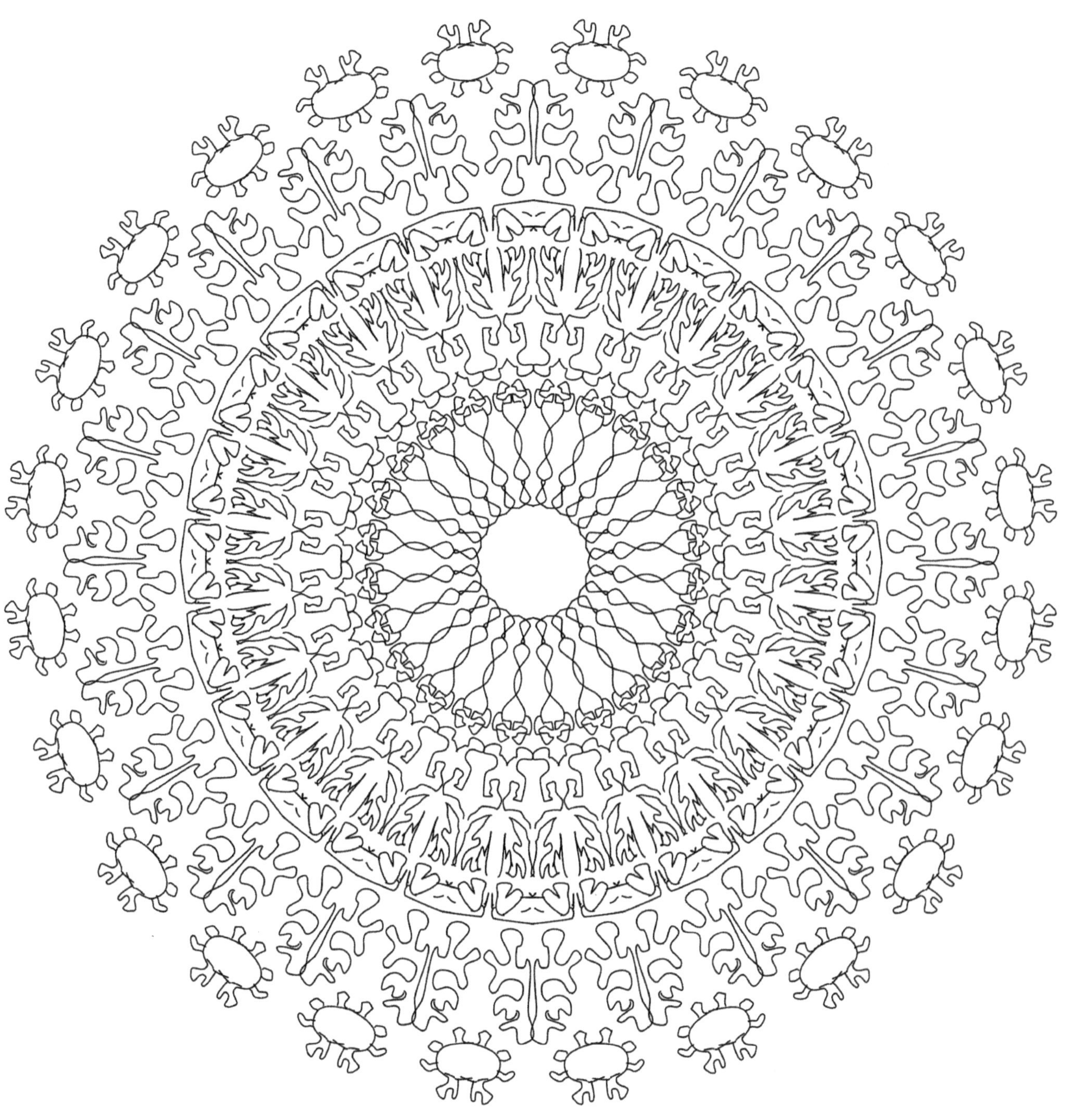

"The clearest way
into the
Universe
is through a forest
wilderness."

~John Muir

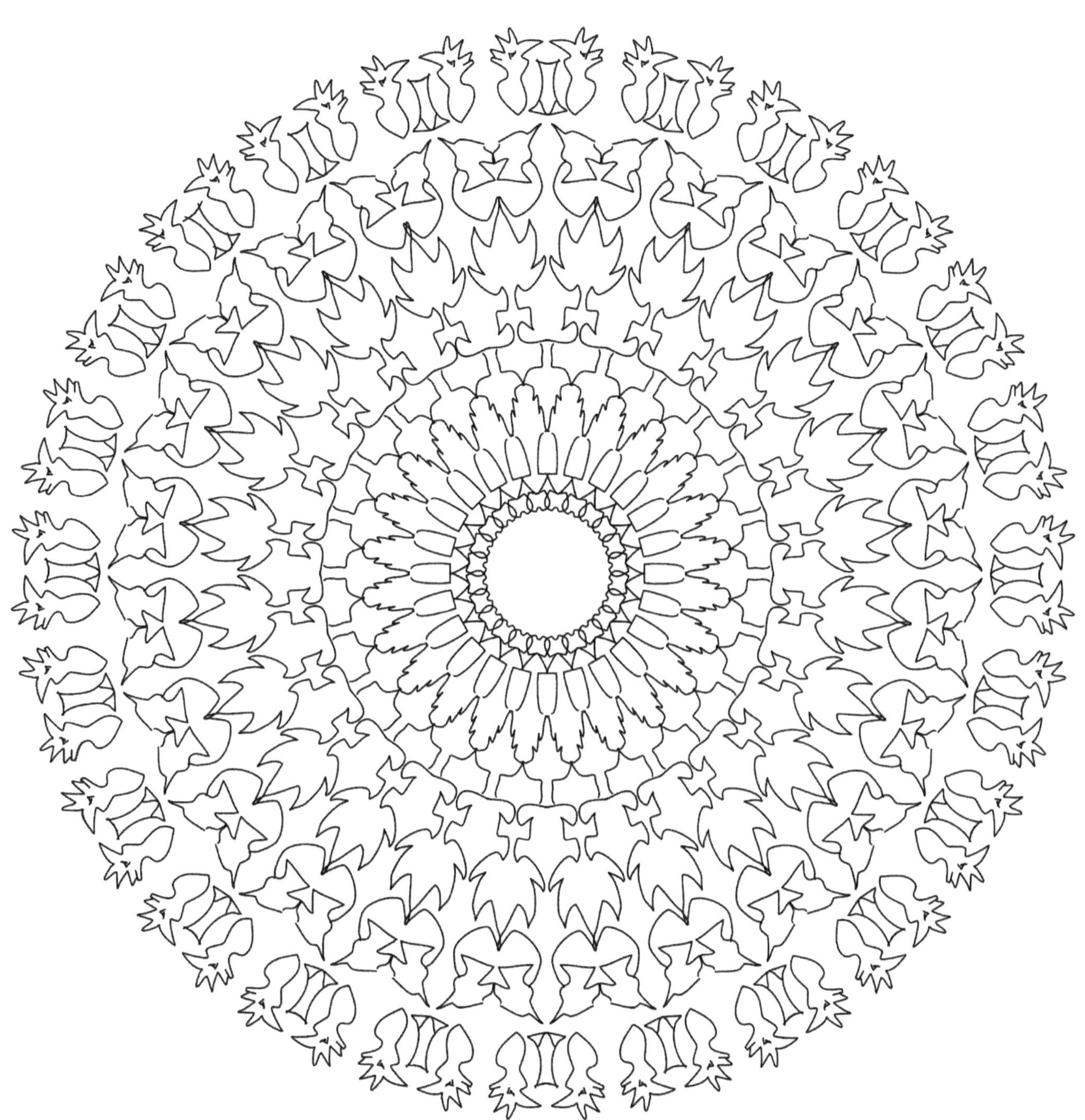